Justice & Liberty For All
A Chapter Book About Supreme Court Cases That Changed America
Joseline Jean-Louis Hardrick

While every precaution has been taken in the preparation of this book, the publisher assumes no responsibility for errors or omissions, or for damages resulting from the use of the information contained herein.

JUSTICE & LIBERTY FOR ALL - A CHAPTER BOOK ABOUT SUPREME COURT CASES THAT CHANGED AMERICA

First edition. April 28, 2025.

Copyright © 2025 Joseline Hardrick.

ISBN: 978-1958912546

Written by Joseline Hardrick.

To the future of America, it's up to you now!

Chapter 1

The Law in Our Lives

The morning sun blazed bright over Bayview Academy for Criminal Justice. It was just after first bell, and a group of seventh graders shuffled into Room 204, the smell of coffee and copy paper filling the air. Their teacher, Ms. Taylor, stood by the whiteboard, her hair twisted into neat dreadlocks, a stack of colorful folders in her hand.
"Morning, everyone!" she called, flashing her usual bright smile.
"Morning, Ms. Taylor!" the class echoed, some sleepy, some wired from breakfast Pop-Tarts.
Ms. Taylor tapped the board where she had written today's agenda: What does justice mean to YOU?
Jaylen, who sat near the window, raised his hand first. "Justice is when the bad guys get locked up," he said confidently.
Across the room, Aisha made a face. "Not always," she said. "Sometimes good people get locked up too. Or people who didn't even do anything wrong."
Malik nodded. "My uncle's a cop. He says it's complicated. People think it's easy, but when you're out there on the street, it's not black and white."
"Yeah," added Sofia from the front row. "My cousin got stopped by the police just for walking home. He wasn't doing anything."
Ms. Taylor listened carefully, letting the classroom buzz with different voices, different stories. She knew these conversations mattered. Here in Tampa Bay—like everywhere—young people were already carrying real experiences with justice and injustice, pride and fear, fairness and unfairness.
She clapped her hands once to get their attention.

"You're all right," she said warmly. "Justice is supposed to mean fairness. But how that looks in real life? Whew—it gets messy."
She picked up a big blue book labeled The U.S. Constitution and held it up.
"That's why we're going to study some real Supreme Court cases this semester," she said. "Not just names and dates. The real people. Their real fights. And the real ways their stories still matter to us."
The class leaned in.
"We're going to see how one man standing up for his rights can change the rules for everyone. How one teenager being denied a fair chance can create new protections for the next generation. How people from all backgrounds—Black, White, Asian, Native, immigrant—made history. Sometimes they won. Sometimes they lost. But they all made a difference."
Jaylen grinned. "Like real-life superheroes?"
Ms. Taylor laughed. "Exactly. And guess what? Y'all are part of that story too."
"By the end of this series, you all are going to present all this information to the rest of the school in a fun way in celebration of Law Day."
Sophia shouted; "Like *Hamilton*?"
Mrs. Taylor winked. "Something like that."
She turned back to the board and wrote one more thing:
First Case: Yick Wo v. Hopkins. 1886.
Question: Can a law be unfair even if it looks fair on paper?
As the bell for second period buzzed faintly down the hall, the room filled with excitement. A new kind of adventure was beginning—not about knights and dragons, but laundries, lawyers, police stops, and second chances.
Real battles.
Real heroes.
Real justice.

Chapter 2

Fair for All? – Lee Yick

The next morning, the students buzzed into Room 204 with even more energy. Ms. Taylor already had the day's first slide on the projector:

Yick Wo v. Hopkins (1886)
When the law looks fair but isn't fair at all.

Jaylen leaned over to Malik. "That sounds shady already," he whispered.

Ms. Taylor smiled. "Today, we're traveling back to 1886, to a place called San Francisco, California. Lots of people had moved there to build new lives — Chinese immigrants, European immigrants, people from all over the world. But not everybody got treated the same."

She clicked to the next slide, showing a simple cartoon of a man standing in front of a small wooden building with "Yick Wo Laundry" painted above the door.

"This man," she said, "is named Lee Yick. He ran a laundry — you know, a place that washed clothes — with his business partner Wo Lee because it was one of the few jobs Chinese immigrants were allowed to have back then."

Sofia raised her hand. "Why just laundries?"

"Because racism," Ms. Taylor said plainly. "Some Americans didn't want Chinese immigrants working in better jobs. They made rules to keep them down. And when Chinese workers found ways to survive anyway, people in power started making new rules to shut them out again."

She flipped to the next slide showing a big official-looking piece of paper. "Here's what happened. San Francisco passed a law saying you needed a 'special permit' to run a wooden laundry. Sounds fair, right?"

The class nodded.

"But here's the catch," Ms. Taylor continued. "When Chinese-owned businesses like Yick Wo applied for the permits — even though they ran clean, safe laundries — the city always said 'NO.' But when White-owned businesses applied for the exact same permits? 'YES.'"

The class murmured.

"Wait—that's totally unfair!" said Brianna from the back.

"Exactly," said Ms. Taylor. "The law didn't say 'only White people allowed.' But the way it was used was racist."
Aisha raised her hand. "So what did Lee Yick do?"
Ms. Taylor grinned. "He and his partner fought back. They said, 'If you say everyone needs a permit, then you have to treat everyone the same when they ask for one.' They took the case all the way to the Supreme Court."
"And they won?" asked Malik, leaning forward.
Ms. Taylor clicked to a final slide:
> **Supreme Court Decision: Laws that are applied unfairly violate the 14th Amendment.**

"Yick Wo won," she said proudly. "The Court said that even if a law looks neutral, if it's used in a racist or unfair way, it's unconstitutional."
The class broke into a small cheer.
Sofia looked thoughtful. "But stuff like that still happens today, right?"
Ms. Taylor nodded. "It does. And that's why we learn these stories. Not because the fight ended—but because it's still going."
She passed out a simple worksheet with one big question at the top:
> *If you see something unfair happening to someone else, what could you do about it?*

As students bent over their papers, the classroom felt different — heavier, but stronger too.
Justice wasn't some faraway thing. It started right where they sat.
And they were just getting started.

Chapter 3

Everyone Needs a Lawyer – Clarence Gideon

The next Monday, Ms. Taylor walked into class holding a thick yellow envelope.

She placed it on the table with a thud.

"This," she said dramatically, "is the most important thing you have if you ever get into trouble."

Everyone stared. Jaylen whispered, "Is it...money?"

Ms. Taylor laughed. "Good guess. But no. It's a lawyer."

She clicked the projector to a new name:

Gideon v. Wainwright (1963)
Even if you're broke, you still deserve help.

The first picture showed a man in ragged clothes holding a crumpled piece of paper.

"This man," she said, "is Clarence Earl Gideon. He didn't have fancy suits. He didn't have a college degree. And when he got accused of stealing from a pool hall in Florida, he didn't have a lawyer either."

Malik frowned. "They didn't give him a lawyer?"

"Nope," Ms. Taylor said. "Florida back then only gave free lawyers for big cases—like murder. So Gideon had to defend himself. No training, no experience, just standing in front of a judge, alone."

Sofia wrinkled her nose. "That's like trying to fly a plane without ever taking a lesson."

"Exactly," Ms. Taylor said. "And guess what? He lost. He went to prison."

The class fell silent.

"But," Ms. Taylor continued, "Gideon didn't give up. He wrote a letter to the Supreme Court. By hand. From prison."

She passed around a copy of Gideon's actual letter. The students leaned in to see his rough handwriting and simple words.

"He said, 'It isn't fair to expect poor people to defend themselves against trained lawyers.' And the Supreme Court agreed."

She clicked to the final slide:

Supreme Court Decision: If you can't afford a lawyer, the government must give you one.

Jaylen nodded slowly. "So public defenders started because of him?"

"Exactly," said Ms. Taylor. "Today, if you're charged with a crime and you can't afford an attorney, the court will appoint one for you—for free. All because one poor man fought for himself...and for everyone after him."

Aisha raised her hand. "But sometimes public defenders are still too busy, right?"

Ms. Taylor sighed. "That's true. The system still isn't perfect. But Gideon gave us the first step."

At the end of class, she wrote a big question on the board:

Why is having a lawyer so important when your freedom is at stake?

As the students packed up, Sofia whispered to Brianna, "I'm gonna remember Gideon. If he could stand up for himself, we can too."

Chapter 4

Privacy Matters – Dollree Mapp

The next day, Ms. Taylor had set up a mini-stage at the front of the room. Two chairs and a table sat in the middle, and she had taped a big fake "WARRANT" sign to the wall.

As the students took their seats, she clicked up today's new case:

Mapp v. Ohio (1961)
When police need permission too.

She picked two volunteers: Jaylen to play a "police officer" and Aisha to play "Ms. Mapp."

"Alright, let's see how this would have looked," Ms. Taylor said.

Jaylen knocked loudly on the table pretending it was a door.

"Police! Open up!" he shouted.

Aisha crossed her arms. "You got a warrant?" she said, grinning.

Jaylen held up a fake piece of paper. "Uh...sure?"

The class giggled.

Ms. Taylor paused the scene.

"Okay, now real life. Here's what actually happened," she said, switching the slide.

She showed a picture of Dollree Mapp, a strong-looking Black woman standing proudly in front of her house.

"Ms. Mapp lived in Cleveland, Ohio. One day, police came banging on her door. They said they needed to search her house, but they didn't have a real warrant. She asked to see it. They waved a piece of paper at her—but it wasn't a real warrant. She snatched it and stuffed it in her dress."

The class laughed and clapped.

Ms. Taylor continued, her voice serious now.

"They searched her home anyway—and found things they said were illegal. They arrested her. She was furious. She hadn't agreed to any search."

Sofia raised her hand. "But they didn't have permission! That's like, against the rules."

"Exactly," Ms. Taylor said, clicking to the next slide.

Supreme Court Decision: Evidence found without a real warrant cannot be used in court.
"It's called the Exclusionary Rule," she explained. "If the police break the rules, they can't use what they find against you. Your home, your space—it's supposed to be protected."
Malik tapped his pencil thoughtfully. "But what if the police think something bad is happening?"
Ms. Taylor nodded. "Sometimes they get real warrants. Sometimes there are emergencies. But rules matter because without them, nobody's safe."
Before the bell, she left them with one big question:
Would you be brave enough to say 'no' if the police tried to search your home without permission?
As the students filed out, Jaylen turned to Aisha and said, "Ms. Mapp was a boss. I hope I'd be that brave."
Ms. Taylor smiled quietly behind them.
That's exactly the lesson she wanted them to carry.

Chapter 5

The Whole Truth – John Brady

The next day, Ms. Taylor dimmed the lights and wrote two simple words on the board:
The Truth
She turned to face the class.
"Today's case," she said, "is about something so simple—but so important. Telling the truth. The whole truth. Especially when someone's life is on the line."
She clicked to the first slide:

Brady v. Maryland (1963)
When hiding the truth isn't fair.

A photo of a serious-looking young man appeared on the screen: John Brady.
"John Brady was charged with a terrible crime," Ms. Taylor explained. "But during his trial, the prosecutors—the people trying to prove he was guilty—hid something important."
The students leaned in.
"They had a confession," she said, "from someone else. A confession that said Brady didn't do the worst part of the crime. But they didn't tell him. They didn't tell the jury. They just kept it quiet."
Aisha gasped. "That's cheating!"
"Exactly," Ms. Taylor agreed. "And because Brady didn't know about the confession, he got a much harsher sentence than he might have."
Sofia raised her hand. "But...aren't prosecutors supposed to be fair?"
Ms. Taylor nodded. "They are. They're supposed to seek justice, not just 'win' a case. And the Supreme Court said hiding important evidence is wrong. It's against the Constitution's guarantee of a fair trial."
She clicked to the next slide:

Supreme Court Decision: The government must share evidence that could help a person's defense.

Jaylen shook his head. "If they hide stuff, it's not a real trial. It's just setting people up to lose."

"Exactly," said Ms. Taylor. "And that's why today, prosecutors are required to hand over any evidence they have that could help prove a person's innocence. It's called a Brady violation if they don't."

She handed out a quick role-play worksheet where students had to pretend they were prosecutors and decide whether to turn over certain evidence. (Spoiler: They were supposed to turn it all over!)

Before the bell rang, she asked:

Why is it important for everyone—especially the government—to tell the whole truth?

As the students packed up, Jaylen muttered, "If they didn't have Brady's back, we gotta have each other's."

Ms. Taylor smiled. The seeds were growing.

Chapter 6

Words That Shouldn't Count - James Wah Toy

On Monday, the classroom was a little noisy — kids were chatting about the cases they had learned so far.
Ms. Taylor clapped her hands once to settle them down.
"Alright, today's case is about how important it is to make sure confessions — and all evidence — are gathered the right way."
She clicked up a new slide:

Wong Sun v. United States (1963)
You can't build justice on broken rules.

A photo appeared of a Chinese-American man named James Wah Toy, standing proudly but quietly in an old black-and-white photo.
"Here's what happened," Ms. Taylor said. "Police thought Wong Sun might be involved in selling drugs. But when they first barged into another man's home—James Wah Toy—they didn't have a proper warrant or real cause."
Aisha frowned. "Wait—again with no warrant?"
"Exactly," said Ms. Taylor. "They scared Toy into giving them names. Then they barged into Wong Sun's house too. They arrested him. They found some things they said were evidence. Later, Wong Sun even made a confession."
Jaylen raised his hand. "So...he admitted it?"
Ms. Taylor nodded. "He said some things—but after being illegally arrested. That's the key."
She clicked the next slide:

Supreme Court Decision: Evidence gained after illegal arrests can't be used in court.

"The Court ruled that when police break the rules at the start—no warrant, no reason—everything that happens after is tainted. It's called the fruit of the poisonous tree."
Sofia's eyes widened. "That sounds serious."
"It is," said Ms. Taylor. "If you let bad arrests stand, you encourage more bad arrests. Justice can't grow from a poisoned tree."
Malik asked, "But what if someone's really guilty?"

Ms. Taylor smiled. "Good question. The Court said even guilty people have rights. And the government has to play fair. Otherwise, we don't have justice. We just have power."

Before the bell rang, she left them with today's big question:

Why is it important to follow the rules, even when you're trying to catch someone who might have done something wrong?

As they packed up, Jaylen muttered, "If you cheat to win...did you really win?"

Ms. Taylor beamed.

Exactly the lesson she wanted them to see.

Chapter 7

Know Your Rights - Ernesto Miranda

The next morning, when the students filed into Room 204, Ms. Taylor had a surprise: she was playing a clip from a TV show where a police officer arrested someone and said the famous words:
"You have the right to remain silent..."
Jaylen's eyes lit up. "Hey! I know that part!"
Sofia nodded. "That's what they always say when someone gets arrested!"
Ms. Taylor smiled and paused the video.
"Yep. Those words? They come from today's case."
She clicked to the next slide:

Miranda v. Arizona (1966)
You need to know your rights.

She pulled up a picture of a young Latino man: Ernesto Miranda.
"Miranda was arrested in Arizona," Ms. Taylor explained. "He didn't really understand what was going on. He didn't know he had the right to stay silent. He didn't know he could ask for a lawyer. So, when the police questioned him for hours, he confessed."
Aisha looked worried. "But what if he didn't know he could say no?"
"Exactly," Ms. Taylor said. "That's why the Supreme Court said: Before questioning someone, police must tell them about their rights."
She clicked to a new slide showing the full Miranda Warning:

- You have the right to remain silent.
- Anything you say can be used against you in court.
- You have the right to a lawyer.
- If you can't afford a lawyer, one will be provided.

The class read it together like a pledge.
Malik raised his hand. "So what happens if they don't say it?"
She clicked to the next slide:

Supreme Court Decision: Defendants have a right to know that they can stay silent and have a lawyer before being questioned.

"Good question," Ms. Taylor said. "If police don't read you your rights before questioning you, your answers might not be allowed in court."

Brianna frowned. "But what if people are scared and just talk anyway?"
Ms. Taylor nodded. "That's why knowing your rights is so important. Even if you're scared. Even if you're confused. You always have the right to stay silent and ask for a lawyer."
She handed out a mini-script so students could act out arrest scenes. (Everyone wanted to be the one reading the Miranda rights.)
Before the bell rang, she left them with a big reminder:

Knowing your rights isn't just for grown-ups. It's for everyone. Including you.

As they packed up their backpacks, Sofia whispered, "I'm gonna practice saying it. Just in case."
Ms. Taylor smiled. That's exactly what she hoped for.

Chapter 8

Lineups and Lawyers – Billy Joe Wade

The next day, Ms. Taylor dimmed the lights and put up a slide that showed a row of cartoon people standing in front of a height chart — like in the movies.

Jaylen grinned. "Oooh, like a police lineup!"

Ms. Taylor nodded.

"Exactly. But today's case shows why lineups have to be fair—and why lawyers matter even there."

She clicked the next slide:

United States v. Wade (1967)
Protecting fairness when memories are fragile.

"This is Billy Joe Wade," Ms. Taylor said, showing a photo of a White man standing stiffly in front of a blank wall.

"He was arrested for robbing a bank. The police put him in a lineup, and witnesses picked him out."

Aisha raised her hand. "But what's wrong with that?"

Ms. Taylor explained, "The problem was... Wade's lawyer wasn't there. And lineups can be super unfair if no one is watching how they're done. Sometimes, police accidentally—or on purpose—give hints about who they think is guilty."

Sofia's eyes widened. "Like...nodding toward someone?"

"Exactly!" Ms. Taylor said. "Or putting one person in different clothes. Or making a suspect stand out in some way."

She clicked to the next slide:

Supreme Court Decision: Defendants have a right to have a lawyer at lineups after being charged.

"The Court said that because lineups are so important—and mistakes can happen so easily—everyone deserves a lawyer's protection during those moments too."

Malik raised his hand. "So... if you don't have a lawyer there, the whole lineup might not be fair?"

"Exactly," said Ms. Taylor. "Memory is tricky. Pressure is real. And fairness has to be built into every step."

Before the bell, she left them with today's big reflection:
How can a small unfair moment change a whole case—and a whole life?
As they packed up, Brianna said thoughtfully, "I never thought about how easy it is for someone to get it wrong. A little thing could mess up someone's whole future."
Ms. Taylor nodded.
"That's why in the law, the little things matter just as much as the big ones."

Chapter 9

Reasonable Suspicion – John Terry

That Thursday, Ms. Taylor had taped two footprints on the classroom floor, leading toward a fake jewelry store sign she made out of cardboard. The students looked curious.

"Today," she said, "we're talking about Terry v. Ohio—a case about police stops, suspicion, and your rights on the street."

She clicked to the slide:

Terry v. Ohio (1968)
When can police stop and frisk you?

Ms. Taylor picked two students: Malik and Jaylen.

"Malik, you're Officer McFadden. Jaylen, you're Terry."

Jaylen started pacing near the jewelry store sign, pretending to look through the window. Malik watched him closely, eyebrows raised.

After a minute, Malik said, "Excuse me, sir, can you step over here?" He patted Jaylen's pockets and pretended to find something.

The class giggled, but Ms. Taylor raised her hand. "Freeze right there. That's pretty close to what actually happened."

She showed them a real photo of John Terry, a Black man in Cleveland, and a reenactment of Officer McFadden's "stop and frisk."

"Officer McFadden thought Terry and his friend looked suspicious. He thought they were 'casing' the jewelry store—checking it out before robbing it. He didn't have a warrant. He didn't see a crime happen. But he had a hunch."

Jaylen frowned. "A hunch? That's it?"

"Yep," Ms. Taylor said. "And he patted Terry down. Found a weapon. Arrested him."

She clicked to the next slide:

Supreme Court Decision: Police can stop and frisk someone based on reasonable suspicion, not full probable cause.

Sofia raised her hand. "But what's 'reasonable suspicion' even mean?"

Ms. Taylor nodded. "That's the tricky part. It's less than proof, but more than just a guess. It's based on an officer's experience and what they observe."

Aisha crossed her arms. "Seems easy to say 'I was suspicious' just because of how someone looks."

"That's a real concern," Ms. Taylor agreed. "This decision gave police more power to stop people. Some say it keeps people safe. Others say it leads to unfair profiling—especially against Black and Brown people."

She handed out a worksheet where students had to decide: When is a stop reasonable? When is it not?

Before the bell, she left them with a big question:

How do we balance safety and freedom?

As they packed up, Jaylen said quietly, "Sometimes the people with badges get to decide—and that's scary."

Ms. Taylor wrote his words on the board: Who gets to decide?

Because that question would keep coming up — again and again.

Chapter 10

A Jury of Your Peers – Gary Duncan

On Friday morning, Ms. Taylor greeted the class with a smile—and a big poster taped to the wall that said:

Would you rather trust one judge...or a jury of people like you?

Jaylen read it out loud and said, "Hmm. Depends who's on the jury!"

The whole class laughed.

Ms. Taylor clicked the projector to a new case:

Duncan v. Louisiana (1968)
The right to a jury trial.

A photo popped up of a young Black man, smiling slightly but standing stiffly: Gary Duncan.

"This," Ms. Taylor said, "is Gary Duncan. He was just 19 years old when he got in trouble in Louisiana. He saw two White boys picking on his younger Black cousins. He stepped in to break it up—touched one of the boys lightly on the arm."

She paused. "Guess what happened?"

Sofia's eyes widened. "They arrested him, didn't they?"

"Yep," Ms. Taylor said. "They charged him with battery—even though nobody was hurt."

The class groaned.

"But when Gary asked for a jury trial—a trial where a group of regular people would hear the case—the court said no. Louisiana didn't have to give him a jury, they said, because it wasn't a 'serious' crime."

Malik shook his head. "Sounds like they just wanted to control it."

Ms. Taylor nodded. "Gary Duncan knew that without a jury, he wouldn't stand a chance in front of a judge who might already be biased against him because of his skin color."

She clicked to the next slide:

Supreme Court Decision: People charged with serious crimes have a right to a jury trial.

"The Court said that the right to a jury trial is too important. It helps protect people from unfair treatment, especially in communities where bias is a real thing."

Jaylen raised his hand. "But what if you don't want a jury?"
"Good question," Ms. Taylor said. "You can give up your right if you want. But the important thing is—it's your choice. Not the government's."
Before the bell rang, she wrote today's big reflection on the board:
Why do you think juries are important for fairness?
As they packed up, Brianna whispered to Sofia, "I'm glad people like Duncan didn't just give up. If he hadn't fought, a lot more people would be stuck with unfair trials today."
Ms. Taylor watched them go, proud.
Every step, they were seeing justice—and their power—more clearly.

Chapter 11

A Good Lawyer Matters - David Washington

When the students arrived on Monday, Ms. Taylor had two chairs facing each other at the front of the classroom. On one chair sat a stuffed bear wearing a sign that said "Defense Lawyer." The other chair was empty except for a crumpled notepad.

The students laughed.

"What happened to the lawyer?" Jaylen joked.

Ms. Taylor grinned. "Exactly the right question. Because today's case is about what happens when you have a lawyer...who doesn't really do their job."

She clicked the projector:

Strickland v. Washington (1984)
When you need a lawyer who fights for you.

The photo on the screen was of David Leroy Strickland, a man who had been sentenced to death after a trial where his lawyer barely even tried to defend him.

"Strickland's lawyer didn't call witnesses. Didn't investigate the case. Didn't even make a closing argument," Ms. Taylor explained.

"He just...gave up."

Sofia frowned. "That's like not even showing up to play."

"Exactly," said Ms. Taylor. "When you're fighting for your life, you deserve a lawyer who actually tries."

She clicked to the next slide:

Supreme Court Decision: Defendants have the right to effective assistance of counsel.

"That means not just any lawyer," she continued. "A real lawyer. Someone who does their homework. Who listens. Who fights."

Aisha raised her hand. "But what if you can't afford a good lawyer?"

Ms. Taylor nodded. "That's still a big problem today. Some public defenders have too many cases. They're overworked. That's why it's important that the law says if your lawyer messes up badly enough, you can challenge your conviction."

Jaylen raised his hand. "So...you have a right to a lawyer—and the right to one who actually cares?"

Ms. Taylor smiled. "Exactly."

Before the bell rang, she left them with today's big reflection:

What makes someone a good defender? What would you want your lawyer to be like?

As the students filed out, Malik muttered, "If I'm ever in trouble, I want a lawyer like a lion—roaring for me."

Ms. Taylor chuckled.

That was a good way to think about it.

Chapter 12

Protecting the Vulnerable – Daryl Atkins

When the students came into Room 204 the next day, Ms. Taylor had a new quote written on the board:
"Justice must be fair, even when it's hard."
She smiled as they took their seats.
"Today's case," she said, "is about a question that's tougher than most: What happens when someone who commits a crime doesn't fully understand right from wrong?"
She clicked the projector:

Atkins v. Virginia (2002)
The death penalty and people with disabilities.

A photo appeared of Daryl Renard Atkins, a young Black man who had been sentenced to death after committing a terrible crime.
"But Atkins had something important that many people missed at first," Ms. Taylor said. "He had an intellectual disability. His mind didn't work the same way. He didn't fully understand the world the way others do."
Sofia raised her hand. "But he still did something bad?"
Ms. Taylor nodded. "Yes. And he had to face the consequences. But the question the Court asked was: Is it fair—or cruel—to execute someone who can't fully understand their actions or defend themselves?"
She clicked the next slide:

Supreme Court Decision: It is unconstitutional to execute people with intellectual disabilities.

Malik leaned forward. "So...they're still responsible, but they deserve mercy?"
"Exactly," Ms. Taylor said. "The Court said that fairness isn't just about punishing wrong. It's about recognizing when someone's abilities mean they deserve a different kind of justice."
Jaylen looked thoughtful. "It's like...the system has to be smarter than just 'hurt them back.'"
"Right," said Ms. Taylor. "Justice isn't about revenge. It's about doing what's right—even when it's hard."
She passed out a short worksheet with this big reflection question:

How should a fair system treat people who struggle to understand right and wrong?
As the bell rang, Sofia whispered, "Justice is bigger than just rules, huh?"
Ms. Taylor smiled wide.
"Exactly. It's about heart, too."

Chapter 13

Rights Even in Wartime – Yaser Hamdi

When Ms. Taylor walked into Room 204 that morning, she was holding a small American flag in one hand—and a handwritten sign in the other that said:
Rights don't disappear during fear.
The students looked curious.
"Today's story," she said, "starts during a scary time—right after 9/11, when everyone was afraid of terrorist attacks. The government made a lot of fast decisions to keep the country safe. But sometimes, in fear, we forget fairness."
She clicked the projector:

Hamdi v. Rumsfeld (2004)
Can the government lock you up without a trial?

A photo popped up of Yaser Hamdi, a U.S. citizen who was captured overseas and brought back to America.
"Here's what happened," Ms. Taylor explained.
"The government said Hamdi was an 'enemy combatant'—someone fighting against America. They put him in military jail. No lawyer. No charges. No trial."
Sofia gasped. "But he's American! Doesn't he have rights?"
"Exactly," Ms. Taylor said. "That's the question the Supreme Court had to answer. Can fear make the Constitution disappear?"
She clicked the next slide:

Supreme Court Decision: Even in wartime, American citizens have the right to due process.

Jaylen raised his hand. "What's due process again?"
Ms. Taylor smiled. "Due process means you have the right to hear the charges against you, to defend yourself, and to have a fair trial before losing your freedom."
Brianna frowned. "So the government can't just say 'you're dangerous' and lock you up forever?"
"Right," said Ms. Taylor. "Not even during war. Not even when people are scared."

She passed around a copy of part of the Court's decision—written in plain language—and asked the students to highlight the words freedom, trial, and rights.

Before the bell rang, she left them with today's reflection:

Why is it important to protect rights even when everyone is afraid?

As they packed up, Malik whispered, "Rights are easy to say we believe in when everything's normal. Harder when it's scary."

Ms. Taylor nodded.

And that was exactly the lesson.

Chapter 14

Immigration and the Law – Jose Padilla

When the students walked into Room 204, Ms. Taylor had a simple sentence on the board:
One bad decision can change your whole life.
The room got quiet. Everyone seemed to feel it.
Ms. Taylor clicked the projector:

Padilla v. Kentucky (2010)
The right to good advice before pleading guilty.

She pulled up a picture of a middle-aged man with tired eyes: Jose Padilla, a U.S. permanent resident from Honduras who had lived in America for decades—served in the U.S. Army, even fought in Vietnam. "Padilla was accused of carrying drugs," Ms. Taylor said. "When he asked his lawyer if pleading guilty would hurt his immigration status, the lawyer said, 'Don't worry about it.'"

Jaylen frowned. "Wait. Was that true?"

Ms. Taylor shook her head. "Nope. It was wrong. Really wrong. Because of that guilty plea, Padilla faced automatic deportation. He was about to be kicked out of the only home he had known for 40 years."

Malik slammed his hand lightly on his desk. "That's not fair! His lawyer set him up!"

Ms. Taylor nodded. "Exactly. And that's why he fought back. He said: If my lawyer gives me bad advice—especially about something this important—that's not real justice."

She clicked to the next slide:

Supreme Court Decision: Lawyers must tell clients if pleading guilty could cause deportation.

"Now," Ms. Taylor said, "because of Padilla, lawyers must talk about immigration consequences clearly. Because the stakes are too high."

Sofia raised her hand. "But what if someone doesn't even know to ask?"

Ms. Taylor nodded. "That's why it's important to have good lawyers—and to be brave enough to ask questions."

Before the bell, she gave them today's big reflection:

What should a good lawyer always explain to their client? Why is honesty so important in the law?

As they packed up, Brianna whispered to Aisha, "One wrong word...and your whole life flips upside down."

Ms. Taylor smiled gently. "That's why knowledge—and standing up for yourself—matters so much."

Chapter 15

A Second Chance – Terrence Graham

The next day, Ms. Taylor had drawn a huge chalk heart on the board, cracked right down the middle. In big letters, it said:
Should mistakes at 16 decide your whole life?
The students stared at it, thinking hard.
Ms. Taylor clicked the projector:

Graham v. Florida (2010)
Kids deserve a second chance.

A photo appeared of a young Black teenager: Terrance Graham. He looked serious, with short-cropped hair and sad eyes.
"Terrance Graham," Ms. Taylor began, "was just sixteen when he made a bad choice. He got caught up in a robbery. No one was killed. No one was seriously hurt."
Jaylen leaned forward. "Okay, bad move...but he's a kid."
"Exactly," Ms. Taylor said. "But after a second mistake, Florida's courts decided Terrance was hopeless. They sentenced him to life in prison. No chance for parole. No chance to ever leave."
Sofia gasped. "Forever? Even though he was just a teenager?"
"Yes," Ms. Taylor said. "The state said he was beyond saving. But the Supreme Court asked: Is that fair? Should we throw away a whole life before it's even had a chance to grow?"
She clicked to the next slide:

Supreme Court Decision: No life without parole for minors in non-homicide cases.

The Court ruled that young people must have a chance for release someday—to show they've changed.
Malik raised his hand. "Because kids can mess up and still turn it around, right?"
Ms. Taylor smiled. "Exactly. Mistakes don't have to be forever. Growth is real. Hope is real."
She passed out a simple question on a half-sheet of paper:
Why do young people deserve second chances?

As the students scribbled thoughtful answers, Brianna whispered, "I'm glad someone believed in him. Everybody deserves a shot to be better." Ms. Taylor nodded quietly.

Justice wasn't just about punishment. It was about hope.

Chapter 16

Our Turn – Law Day Musical!

May 1st finally arrived—Law Day—and Room 204 was buzzing like a beehive.

The gym at Bayview Academy had been transformed into a real stage:

- Bright banners hung overhead that read "Justice & Liberty for All!"

- Chairs lined up neatly for parents, teachers, and even some local police officers and judges who came to watch.

- Students hurried back and forth, adjusting costumes and setting up simple props, such as gavels, doors, and a giant paper "Constitution" on the back wall.

Backstage, Ms. Taylor gathered her class for a pep talk.
She looked out at her kids—some nervous, some excited, some bouncing in place—and felt a swell of pride.
"You," she said, voice steady and warm, "are about to teach everyone something bigger than laws and rules. You're going to show them what justice means when real people fight for it. You're telling the stories of hope, courage, and change."
Jaylen whispered to Sofia, "I feel like a real history-maker."
"You ARE," Ms. Taylor said, overhearing him.
The music started—the opening beats of their original Justice & Liberty: The Musical—and one by one, the students stepped onto the stage.

- Jaylen as Yick Wo, fighting unfair rules.
- Aisha as Dollree Mapp, standing strong at her door.
- Malik as Terrance Graham, singing about second chances.
- Sofia as Ernesto Miranda, learning to use her voice.
- Brianna as Gary Duncan, demanding a fair jury.

Each scene showed a different case, woven together with music, laughter, powerful speeches, and even a few tears.

Parents wiped their eyes. Officers nodded thoughtfully. Judges clapped with real emotion.

The message rang loud and clear: Justice wasn't something that just happened in old history books. Justice was a living, breathing promise. And it needed everyone's voice.

At the final song, the whole class stood together under the giant "Constitution" sign, fists raised high, singing:

> ***"We are the ones who will carry the flame,***
> ***Fighting for freedom, not fortune or fame.***
> ***Justice and liberty, standing so tall,***
> ***The promise is ours—to protect it for all!"***

The gym exploded into cheers.

Ms. Taylor clapped the hardest of all, tears in her eyes.

Because she knew, these students weren't just acting.

They were becoming.

They were becoming the next guardians of justice.

And this... was just their beginning.

Chapter 17

The Constitution Behind It All

After the Law Day show, Ms. Taylor gathered the class one last time. "You did an amazing job," she said, her voice full of pride. "But before we wrap up, I want to show you the roots that connected all these cases together."

She pulled down a giant poster of the Bill of Rights and the Fourteenth Amendment, taping them to the board.

"Every case you performed," Ms. Taylor said, "was about these words. These promises. Let's go over them together."

She clicked up a new slide:

Fourth Amendment – Protecting Privacy

"The right of the people to be secure...against unreasonable searches and seizures."

What it means:

The police can't search your stuff, your home, or you without a good reason and usually a warrant.

Cases we learned:

- *Mapp v. Ohio* – Can't use evidence from illegal searches.
- *Terry v. Ohio* – Police need "reasonable suspicion" to frisk you.

Fifth Amendment – Fair Treatment

"No person shall...be compelled in any criminal case to be a witness against himself."

What it means:

You don't have to say anything that could get you in trouble (the right to remain silent).

Cases we learned:

- *Miranda v. Arizona* – You must be told your rights when arrested.
- *Brady v. Maryland* – The government must share helpful evidence.

Sixth Amendment – The Right to a Fair Trial
"In all criminal prosecutions, the accused shall enjoy the right...to have the assistance of counsel for his defense."
What it means:
You have the right to a lawyer, a fair and public trial, and to know what you're accused of.
Cases we learned:

- *Gideon v. Wainwright* – If you can't afford a lawyer, one will be given to you.

- *Brady v. Maryland* – Prosecutors must tell the defendant If they find out helpful evidence for their case.

- *United States v. Wade* – You have a right to a lawyer at important parts of your case, like lineups.

- *Duncan v. Louisiana* – You have the right to a jury trial in serious cases.

- *Strickland v. Washington* – You have a right to a lawyer who tries their best and puts on a defense.

- *Padilla v. Kentucky* – Lawyers must give good advice, especially about immigration consequences.

Eighth Amendment – No Cruel or Unusual Punishment
"Excessive bail shall not be required...nor cruel and unusual punishments inflicted."
What it means:
Punishments must be fair, not too harsh or extreme.
Cases we learned:

- *Atkins v. Virginia* – You can't execute people with intellectual disabilities.

- *Graham v. Florida* – Kids can't be sentenced to life without parole for non-murder crimes.

Fourteenth Amendment – Equal Protection and Fair Process
"No state shall...deprive any person of life, liberty, or property, without due process of law; nor deny...the equal protection of the laws."

What it means:
Everyone must be treated equally and fairly, no matter what.
Cases we learned:

- *Yick Wo v. Hopkins* – Laws must be applied fairly to everyone.
- *Wong Sun v. United States* – Evidence gained unfairly can't be used.
- *Hamdi v. Rumsfeld* – Even in wartime, citizens deserve a fair trial.

Ms. Taylor smiled as she finished.
"Each amendment," she said, "is like a shield. Every time someone stood up in court, they helped make that shield stronger—for all of us."
The students nodded, some even clapping softly.
Justice wasn't just about big moments. It was about protecting little rights every single day.
And now, thanks to their journey, they knew those rights belonged to them too.
THE END!

Author's Note

Take middle-grade readers on an unforgettable journey through the real stories behind America's most important Supreme Court cases with *Justice & Liberty: A Chapter Book About Supreme Court Cases That Changed America*

Told through the lens of a middle-school class of students from diverse backgrounds learning Constitutional Law, this chapter book dives deep into civics education while connecting history to today's world.

Perfect for celebrating Law Day, Constitution Day, Career Day, Bring Your Child to Work Day, Great American Teach-In, Juneteenth, and Independence Day, this book is a must-read for young activists, future lawyers, and families passionate about fairness.

Recommended for programs supported by the American Constitution Society, Federalist Society, and all who believe in empowering youth through the U.S. Constitution.

The images in this book are artistic representations meant to reflect the spirit, traits, and diversity of the real people and events. They are *not exact portraits* of any individual. I use some abstract and symbolic styles to honor the meaning of each story, focusing on the larger ideas of justice, courage, and fairness that these individuals represent.

Glossary of Justice Terms

Amendment
A change or addition to the U.S. Constitution. It protects people's rights.
Appeal
Asking a higher court to review and change a lower court's decision.
Bill of Rights
The first 10 amendments to the U.S. Constitution, listing important rights like freedom of speech and the right to a fair trial.
Due Process
Fair treatment through the normal legal system, especially when someone is accused of a crime.
Equal Protection
The idea that everyone must be treated equally under the law, no matter who they are.
Exclusionary Rule
A rule that says evidence collected illegally can't be used in court.
Jury
A group of regular people who listen to a trial and decide if someone is guilty or not.
Lineup
A police procedure where a witness looks at several people to try and identify someone who committed a crime.
Miranda Rights
The rights police must tell you about when you're arrested—like staying silent and asking for a lawyer.
Probable Cause
Strong reasons to believe that someone has broken the law.
Reasonable Suspicion

A small but smart reason police can stop and briefly search someone if they think something is wrong.
Search Warrant
A document from a judge that lets police search a person's home or property.
Self-Incrimination
Saying something that can be used against you in court. You have the right to stay silent to avoid it.
Supreme Court
The highest court in the United States. It makes final decisions about laws and rights.
Unconstitutional
Against what the Constitution allows.

Don't miss out!

Visit the website below and you can sign up to receive emails whenever Joseline Hardrick publishes a new book. There's no charge and no obligation.

https://books2read.com/r/B-A-WLGV-ZXRGG

BOOKS 2 READ

Connecting independent readers to independent writers.

About the Author

Empowering Every Legal Journey™

At Lawyerish® we empower the next generation of legal professionals.

We are dedicated to providing resources, insights, and inspiration for those who are law-adjacent and anyone aspiring to make a positive impact in the legal field.

Read more at https://thelawyerish.com/.

About the Publisher

Lawyerish®

Empowering Every Legal Journey™

At Lawyerish®, we empower the next generation of legal professionals by meeting them where they are and guiding them to where they want to go. Connect with us at lawyerish.org. Lawyerish® is a registered trademark of Twelve:Two Training, LLC.

Read more at https://www.lawyerish.org.